Exploring Job Skills

by Stuart Schwartz and Craig Conley

Content Consultant:
Robert J. Miller, Ph.D.
Associate Professor
Mankato State University

C APSTONE
H IGH/L OW B OOKS
an imprint of Capstone Press

C A P S T O N E   P R E S S
818 North Willow Street • Mankato, MN 56001
http://www.capstone-press.com

Copyright © 1998 Capstone Press. All rights reserved.
No part of this book may be reproduced without written permission from the publisher.
The publisher takes no responsibility for the use of any of the materials
or methods described in this book, nor for the products thereof.
Printed in the United States of America.

Library of Congress Cataloging-in-Publication Data
Schwartz, Stuart, 1945-
    Exploring job skills/by Stuart Schwartz and Craig Conley.
    p. cm. -- (Looking at work)
    Includes bibliographical references and index.
    Summary: Describes how to determine, evaluate, utilize, and improve job skills.
    ISBN 1-56065-712-X
    1. Vocational guidance--Juvenile literature. [1. Vocational guidance.] I. Conley, Craig, 1965-   . II. Title. III. Series: Schwartz, Stuart, 1945-   Looking at work.
HF5381.2.S38 1998
650.1--dc21
                                        97-53217
                                        CIP
                                        AC

Photo credits:
All photos by Dede Smith Photography

Table of Contents

Chapter 1 Exploring Job Skills 5
Chapter 2 Reading 7
Chapter 3 Writing 9
Chapter 4 Math 11
Chapter 5 Computer Skills 13
Chapter 6 Listening 15
Chapter 7 Speaking 17
Chapter 8 Manual Dexterity 19
Chapter 9 Creative Thinking 21
Chapter 10 Decision Making 23
Chapter 11 Problem Solving 25
Chapter 12 Job Skills and You 27

Words to Know 28
To Learn More 29
Useful Addresses 30
Internet Sites 31
Index 32

Exploring Job Skills

Many people want to find good jobs. They can start by exploring and improving their job skills.

Employers hire workers who have good job skills. An employer is a person or company that hires and pays workers. Workers must have certain job skills for each job.

Most workers must be able to read and write. They should be able to listen well and speak well. Most workers must also have basic math skills.

Some workers also need special skills. These skills help them perform certain jobs. People who work in offices should have computer skills. Construction workers should be skilled at using tools.

People who do not have basic skills can learn them. They can go to school. They can learn from people who have these skills. They can practice skills at home. People who improve their basic skills often find better jobs.

Some workers need special skills.

Chapter 2

Reading

Most workers need to read on the job. They may need to read directions or instructions. Delivery drivers read directions. Directions tell drivers where to go. Hotel clerks read reservations. Reservations tell clerks who will be staying at the hotel.

Some workers must read specifications. Specifications are facts that tell how to build objects. Workers building a house need specifications. The specifications tell how big the house should be. They also tell its shape.

Reading also helps workers learn new skills. Cooks learn to make new foods by reading recipes. Hospital workers read about new ways to help people get well.

Employers know that good readers can learn new things. Workers who read well can keep up with changes on the job.

Most workers need to read on the job.

Chapter 3

Writing

Many workers need to write on the job. Writing helps workers share information with others. Good writing is clear. Other people can read and understand it.

Some people do a lot of writing on the job. Office workers write letters and reports. Police officers write reports about accidents. They write tickets when drivers break the law. Truck drivers keep records of how far they drive. Drivers also write down the goods they haul in their trucks. Food servers write orders for meals.

Some people write to earn a living. Writers work at newspapers and magazines. Authors write books. These people must have strong writing skills.

Police officers write reports about accidents.

Chapter 4

Math

Basic math skills are necessary for most jobs. Workers must know how to add, subtract, multiply, and divide.

Carpenters make objects out of wood. They use math to plan what they will build. They measure the size and shape of wood. Cooks also use math. They measure amounts of food. Cashiers must know how to count money. They must be able to make proper change.

Some people work with numbers to earn a living. They do jobs like bookkeeping. Bookkeepers record how much money companies make and spend. They use math every day.

Some people use math on the job every day.

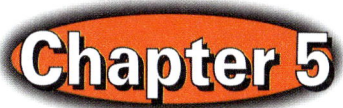

Computer Skills

Many workers need computer skills. They must be able to use different computer programs. Computers help workers do their jobs.

Many companies use computers. Stores use them to keep track of items for sale. Sales clerks use computers to find items they need. Secretaries use computers to create letters and reports.

People learn computer skills in many ways. Some people learn on the job. For example, employers may teach clerks to use their stores' computers. Other people learn computer skills by taking classes. Many schools offer computer classes.

Many libraries have computers, too. People can use these computers for free. They can practice and improve their computer skills.

Computers help workers do their jobs.

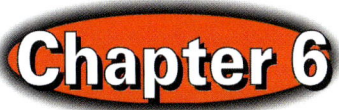

Chapter 6

Listening

Some people do not think of listening as a skill. But listening is an important job skill. People with good listening skills hear what others say. They also understand what others mean.

Many workers must listen closely to other people. For example, child care workers listen to parents. They ask if children need medicine. They learn about special foods children need to eat. Child care workers listen to children, too. They must know if children feel sick or afraid.

Teachers must also listen. They listen to their students. They must understand students' questions so they can provide good answers.

Child care workers listen to children.

Speaking

Speaking is another important job skill. Many workers must give information to other people. They often do this by speaking.

Speaking well helps workers do their jobs. Good speakers help others understand what they say. They speak slowly and clearly. They repeat their words if listeners do not understand. They give more information when others ask questions.

For example, sales clerks use speaking skills to sell things. They talk about the products they sell. Librarians help people find information at the library. They answer questions and tell people how to find books. These people could not do their jobs without speaking skills.

Sales clerks use speaking skills to sell things.

Chapter 8

Manual Dexterity

Many employers hire workers who can use their hands well. The ability to use the hands well is called manual dexterity. People who have manual dexterity can do many jobs. They can work in factories. They can use computers. They can repair machines. They can sew clothing.

Some jobs require manual dexterity. Auto mechanics must have manual dexterity. They must be able to handle small parts of engines. Construction workers must be able to handle tools. Musicians must also have manual dexterity to play their instruments.

People who have manual dexterity can do many jobs.

Chapter 9

Creative Thinking

Good workers often use creative thinking. Creative thinking is thinking in new and useful ways. Workers who use creative thinking can think of better ways to do their work. They can solve problems.

Creative thinking can play a part in every job. A newspaper carrier might think of a faster way to deliver newspapers. A barber could give a customer a new kind of haircut. A baker can create new bread recipes. All these ideas are the result of creative thinking.

Some jobs require creative thinking. A florist arranges flowers. A florist must choose which flowers to use in a flower arrangement. The florist uses creative thinking to make choices. Creative thinking helps the florist put together a beautiful arrangement.

Some jobs require creative thinking.

Chapter 10

Decision Making

Everyone makes decisions on the job. Workers must decide how to spend their time. Some jobs have many duties. Workers must decide which duties to do first.

Good workers consider all their choices before making decisions. They talk with others who can help choose the best decisions. Then they follow through on their decisions.

For example, a housekeeper cleans many areas in a hotel. The front desk is messy. But the rooms need cleaning, too. The housekeeper thinks about where to start cleaning.

The housekeeper decides to start with the front desk. This area is the first area hotel visitors see. Next, the housekeeper asks a clerk which rooms will have guests that night. The housekeeper cleans those rooms. The housekeeper cleans the other rooms last.

Everyone makes decisions on the job.

Chapter 11

Problem Solving

Problem solving is another important job skill. Good problem solvers learn all they can about each problem. Then they use decision making skills to solve the problems.

A bus driver sees that the riders seem angry. The bus driver asks them why they are angry. They say they do not like standing in the wind at the bus stop. The driver sees a problem.

The driver asks if the bus company can build a shelter at the bus stop. The shelter will help riders stay out of the wind. The bus company agrees to build a shelter if 20 riders ask for it.

The driver tells the riders to call the bus company. More than 20 riders call the company to ask for a shelter. The company builds the shelter. The driver has shown good problem solving skills.

Problem solving is an important job skill.

Chapter 12

Job Skills and You

Employers need workers who have job skills. They need workers who can read. They need people who can use math. Employers need workers who can make decisions and solve problems. Many employers need workers who can use creative thinking.

You probably have important job skills. You can improve these skills. You can learn new skills, too.

Schools are good places to learn job skills. You can take classes in reading, writing, math, and computers. Many schools can help you receive loans to pay for the classes.

You can also practice your skills outside of school. Reading for fun helps people read better on the job. Writing letters can help you improve your writing skills. Your public library may have computers you can use. Your skills will improve as you learn. Better skills can help you find better jobs.

Employers need workers who have job skills.

Words to Know

creative thinking (kree-AY-tiv THINGK-ing)—thinking in a new and useful way

decision making (di-SIZH-uhn MAYK-ing)—making a choice

manual dexterity (MAN-yoo-uhl dek-STER-uh-tee)—the ability to use the hands well

specifications (spess-uh-fuh-KAY-shuhnz)—facts that tell how to build objects

To Learn More

McFarland, Rhoda. *The World of Work*. New York: Rosen Publishing Group, 1993.

Schwartz, Stuart and Craig Conley. *Improving Work Habits*. Mankato, Minn.: Capstone High/Low Books, 1998.

Whelchel, Mary. *How to Thrive from Nine to Five*. Dallas: Word Publishing, 1995.

Useful Addresses

Canada WorkInfoNet
Room 2161, Asticou Training Centre
241 Boulevard Citè des Jeunes
Hull, Quebec K1A 0M7
Canada

CoolWorks
P.O. Box 272
Gardiner, MT 59030

Employment and Training Administration
200 Constitution Avenue NW
Room N-4700
Washington, DC 20210

U.S. Department of Labor
Office of Public Affairs
200 Constitution Avenue NW
Room S-1032
Washington, DC 20210

Internet Sites

America's Job Bank
http://www.ajb.dni.us

Pre-employment
http://www.milwaukee.tec.wi.us/esl/
   premply.htm

Skills
http://www.careerlinx.regina.sk.ca/
   empplaza/hiring/skls.htm

Skills Most in Demand by Employers
http://www.utononto.ca/career/skills.htm

Index

computer skills, 5, 13
creative thinking, 21, 27

decision making, 23, 25
directions, 7

employer, 5, 7, 13, 19, 27

instructions, 7

library, 13, 17, 27
listening, 15

manual dexterity, 19
math, 5, 11, 27

problem solving, 25

reading, 7, 27
reservations, 7

school, 4, 13, 27
speaking, 17
specifications, 7

write, 5, 9, 27